REALIZATION

JAMES M SNIPES

Order this book online at www.trafford.com
or email orders@trafford.com

Most Trafford titles are also available at major online book retailers.

Printed in Victoria, BC, Canada.

ISBN: 978-1-4269-2583-2 (Soft)

*Our mission is to efficiently provide the world's finest, most comprehensive
book publishing service, enabling every author to experience success.
To find out how to publish your book, your way, and have it available
worldwide, visit us online at www.trafford.com*

Trafford rev. 02/16/2010

 www.trafford.com

North America & international
toll-free: 1 888 232 4444 (USA & Canada)
phone: 250 383 6864 ♦ fax: 812 355 4082

*This collection of untainted thoughts and raw emotion
is dedicated to the biggest hero's of my life, my father
Michael C. Snipes and my mother Selma D. Snipes.*

Preface

I did not portray these thoughts to capture ignorant media driven eyes, I wrote them for the individuals who possess their own independent thoughts as well as a true and free mind. Within my words you will find anger, blind frustration, confusion and resolution through failed love stories all leading to a perfect realization of whom I have always been underneath the simple character I play everyday. You will also find an observed injustice among planned laws to further a certain control by those of political power. Though such words are opinion based, I am sure anyone can find truth in what I find as an abomination of our so called rights as people. What you will not find is fiction nor a means to sell words in the name of profit. What I hope you will find as the reader is the fact you are not alone in whatever struggle you may face in life as all of us true to ourselves will always find a fight worth dying for and a love worth living for.

Contents

"Freedoms Lost"

Almost helpless at times, we sit blindly in front of the TV watching the life of another, mindless of our own lives. Blinded our eyes have become by the billboard of lights when every passing freedom goes unnoticed as we keep buying the lies and excuses as to why there is yet another law in place of what was once a natural freedom of being human. A constitution of no value is replaced with every new law created to fill the wallet of one who is in power because we are to blind to change a system sold on lies. We are led to believe that we have control of our lives, but every decision made is among the others forced into our minds over and over until the true plan of domination is no longer apparent to the common law-abiding mind. We live our lives the way someone else intended, living under laws created in lies of the better America, the better system of control. Even as I write these words of a bitter truth, they may be shunned out of improper grammar due to a fading freedom of speech and individuality. There must be a certain diversity to separate the degrees of accomplishments and differences that are being stolen to create the better America, the better system of control. Freedom cannot exist in a controlled society full of weak minds being trained from birth to obey these laws no one will ever seem to question. There have been so many lies emerging throughout the years that one tends to forget what that original purpose and truth was. So who really knows what that purpose was in the preface of greed, we can only rely on our true feelings of what should be without the forced thoughts of distraction.

"Political Misery"

The truth becomes blackened with your eyes as the truth of our reality is lost and destroyed just like the dream pushed upon your eyes. My ears go deaf as you proclaim your ignorance. What happens when your God dies within your faults and your vision loses a hope so precious , so real , your speech becomes one of lost integrity. The peoples hopes and dreams are so weak and pointless while you force your greed upon our hearts expecting us to adopt your dreams, your lies for a better country. My mind can only rebel as my skin seems to burn from my bones living a life under such unjust laws, new systems of control thought up everyday by your governing minds. In this mind is hidden the sweetest of things but always cold to this rage I feel so deep within my veins, my blood boils with the thought of living under another's control, another's sense of what life should be. My hope slowly becomes lost as I watch so many others become blind within your speeches your life, lies sold while the truth lied. As one wall crumbles in my mind they all begin to follow remembering all of the failure in my life as I begin to like hating you. My sight is losing touch with reality as I soon only begin to grip this rage letting the pain flood through my veins while the hate keeps building. We are all sacrificed to careless attributes of your better way. As this thought burns through me I feel myself becoming purified rage, sanctified purity, bleeding your eyes to hear my words of doubtfulness, lack of hope. My pain will become your virtue as those crooked lines lead me through your hells . Your hate is justified as mine is viewed as random and pointless through more of your lies. I can only accept this rage as my mind slowly drifts from reality.

"Liberation"

Screaming through the silent rage of a common slave, you destroy yourself each day just to fill the bank account of another greedy company. You sacrifice each day for an ungrateful service just to pay for a natural freedom that steals all that is truly free. Your time and energy wasted, your thoughts forgotten as you live yet another day for someone else, forgetting what that dream first meant to you. Memories soon become replaced with a control so strong that you cannot remember how you became what and where you are. The doubt sets in as fear guides you to the machine of life portrayed through your political leader in bedded upon lies of a free world with an expensive price tag. The bar is set so high; the common mind can only accept what is placed before them granting more strength to the machine built for pure control of the human spirit. Hell truly becomes within a life lived upon this ignorant world when we are forced to live the opinionated failure of another's standard of life. Success is chosen at random to retain a balance that leaves the machine unnoticed and the poor poorer. Broken dreams and forgotten promises pave a road of systematic control for those not chosen in your secret war fought by blind eyes dependant upon this system forged in misery. A nation grown through violence, a country formed through lies, when will we wake up and fight against what we have been blindly fighting for all of these years? When will the body count of lost souls really make enough difference to change the way people think and function everyday? When will we live the original truth that was so apparent before the idea of control became apparent? We must liberate our minds to truly liberate the freedom that has been waiting all along.

"A reaction of hate"

The comforting annoyance of hate seems to be a divine one when looking through your political eyes. I have to remain in denial just to cope with this reality you shove in my face everyday. My eyes burn just to satisfy what I don't want to see, your political indifference among all of our realities. Your blind hate paves the road to an injustice only you could make work, a reality only you would dream of and destroy anyone that you have to just to make it everyone's reality. You make yourself blind to the hearts and lives that you selfishly destroy as you make yourself look justified in the process. Your greed defines your true intentions to create this new system of control that you think everyone will accept. Your fear created laws and so called plans for human growth only fill your pockets, fill your greedy dreams of control and a false happiness. There is one thing you are too blind and selfish to accept, not everyone is blinded by your fictional realities that you give out like a selfish figure of a god and foolishly believe that we will become your zombies to control. Our minds are too strong to fulfill your dreams of control and domination, these worthless powers you crave will never be a fear in our minds. We don't need your donations of minds, almost like a sale of realities to be purchased and not learned, not lived, only playing a part in that hidden system of lies and hate you swear by everyday. Those of us with a mind still left after your constant distractions will not help you to build your kingdom of robots, minds unable to function without your control, without your distractions. You may already have some of the American people in your grasp ready to be controlled but you will not have us all, we will die fighting against your cause and your destruction of the human race. I will watch your selfish dreams of control crumble as you feel completely helpless, the same way you try to make us all feel. Helpless without your system, well we know where your system takes us and we will never accept that reality. Our lives are worth more than you pretend them to be. Your system will never be needed for us to find our own happiness on any level. Those who become lost in life will never need your guidance, our path will be put in front of us all with a choice of unlimited possibilities, something your system could never offer. A certain freedom is growing more real everyday in our hearts and that freedom does not include your laws, your excuse for a better world for we can see straight through your circle of lies. We will rise above as you fall into the hell that you have been trying to drive us into for decades. Your blind hate will swallow your life, your mind and as you crash to the ground the people will realize the life they have missed because they were blinded by your hate. They took it as their own because you always controlled what was seen and felt until the rebellious mind stood up against your system of total control.

"Pain Addict"

You hold the hand of glory to your own suffering and self-pity. All of those glorious moments in your life so short and unappreciated, but in your mind so long and abused, you forget how to live without them. You become the history of what will happen. You watch everyone destroy themselves and wonder if they see the same in your eyes. You still wonder if that door in your mind will ever open and what un-comforting thoughts will flood into your already crowded mind. Your time remains a still one in such a horrid way, you cant help but to worry. Those personal tragedies repeat over and over again, hard to see but still you thought that salvation was just one more tragedy away. Sometimes you enjoy the pain each tragedy brings, but then you feel an immense need for love, a love that will always bring a pain that slowly turns to hate. Soon you fear that you are hate, straight through, straight down. Does your fiction make reality that much easier? Everyday you hope for that one day that you will feel nothing. You become dependent on all that is wrong in hopes that your fiction will become your reality. That fucking change again, always in your head, never bringing a sense of release or happiness. Let go, she will never change to you, the same beautiful face you have always known will be all you ever see in your states of regret and denial. Silent rages are natural, love has to be learned. You begin to realize that you cannot open your mind anymore to her and she is gone but remains enough to remind you of your constant failure and soon that fiction takes over your thoughts again to the pain of reality.

"Dreamscape"

These dreamscapes play with all emotions, all gods and all of those fluttering demons resting in my mind. They remain to be such a familiar pain, very close to heart, very real. Its just a step from reality in my truth but it is a million miles from you, your heart. Why must you be so narrow minded? Its just occupational pain, a constant distress, a role your made to follow. My dreamscape occludes this world from my thoughts except for the occasional beautiful face floating through memory of maybe a wonderful dream I had but these occasional thoughts are always thrown away but sometimes re-opened for viewing. My thoughts are hidden in a mist of words , never to be sought out by the common stare. There are no miracles in this everlasting tragedy. The dreamscape lets me forget the fact that my family is a net for everyone which is falling but we cant seem to let go. Maybe we could try again but it still hurts too much to feel, to see. This emanation of hope in my life you blindly speak of becomes yet another lie. These gates flood open to the blood of innocents raining down within my troubled mind, my endless doubt, my dreamscape.

"Total Attrition"
self salvation

Hate me, then try me, use me, then waist me one more time. Then maybe I will go away, all problems will drift into submission, total attrition and maybe then I can save myself this time. The pitch of your voice, that un-fake smile upon your soft face, the way only you can treat me, all of these things demonstrating your un-dying love of happiness. You seemed so different from the greed driven demon that I hold so close in my mind. It uses me, feeds from these tainted thoughts twisting upon realities roller-coaster of lies and ignorance. Sometimes you fill me with such sweet thoughts and hopes but they always find an end in your un-kept promises. My forgiving hand could guide you among any hard place your life may force you to take alone. I want so much to feel love but this confusion-causing hate creating ignorance is too real and I cannot understand it. This pain blinds me to all that can be and to all that could have been. How could you be so real but so plastic and materialistic? How can you touch me with so many lies?

"Devils Maid"

Maybe I will drown in this chemical induced smoke that I breath as my own. How can you make such beautiful things just to destroy them? I guess nothing is really meant to last. Your eternity becomes a false term as reality sets in. Can you absorb my soul into your grasp as well? This pain engulfed life becomes ever easy to achieve. It seems that sorrow hides behind every door. Im broken and blasted away in such an unbearable manner, into destruction, into delirium. Your desire creates your destiny which ultimately creates your despair. This animosity occurs in my mind through every breath, a roller-coaster ride through heavens most beautiful sites straight down to your self created hell. Once again a beautiful thing aged and taken away before it could be truly alive. Upon the lips of pretty and innocent women the hands of under-achieved men will infest and destroy. Under a cloudless sky, a warm place, rest knowing its downfall is not far behind. Always left there to reconcile as these thoughts sink into a deep abyss of undoubted struggle. Take away this pain and maybe we could live again without the fear of happiness.

"Sometimes, Just somewhere"

Sometimes you find something that you want so much it becomes almost impossible to see anything, the reality of life is soon forgotten. An insightful puzzle your mind will always become when blinded by such a wasted devotion. You become so confused and begin to hate what you cant understand when you forget how to let go of the pain you've grown to live. Sometimes its easier not to start this life over again and go straight for the end, that new reality you crave so dearly. Where is there hope in a life of constant struggle, being let down over and over. Where is there hope when that ending stays so close to mind, so true to heart. Death always screams of agony and life enjoys the pain death carries, but life knows the end is never too far away. Things can always change when a little bit of truth is added to your facts, your lies. What will you do when things cant be seen anymore, when your mind will not automatically fix those problems you ignore everyday?

"Chain Bearer"
(letter to dad)

As I watch the useless suffering of a shadowed up keeper, I begin to notice the still life so apparent in their movement I soon develop paranoia of what I will become as time slowly steals my youth. I begin to let those thoughts flood my mind as my angel sells a thought and lends a lie. The memories follow the thoughts, as they always will, pulling that sadness from the murky waters of his grave reminding me of the tragedy his legacy became. I viewed him as such a lonely man, towards the end anyway, silent heartbeat, misdirected rage, and a love so strong for her, his life became an empty one after that regretful decision. As his life caught up to the end that he was looking for, I realized to late that the ending was death. I was to late to change the outcome, I was to blackened by my own ignorance to see the truth of those clues he set upon only my eyes and that decision became my past before I could open my eyes to his thoughts. I'M SORRY EVERYDAY I WAKE UP, WHEN I TRY TO SPEAK TO MY FATHER, I SOON REALIZE IT WAS ONLY A DREAM, AND HE IS NO LONGER HERE TO SPEAK TO. I'm SORRY I COULD NOT SHOW YOU THE LOVE YOU SHOWED ME WHEN IT WOULD HAVE MATTERED THE MOST. I CAN ONLY HOPE THAT YOU CAN STILL SEE ME, AND I WILL FOREVER FEEL YOU IN EVERY DECISION, AND IN EVERY LIFE I DECIDE TO LIVE. Can you see me now, dad? I'm just like you in such a twisted way, I can begin to see the logic in your decision. I have become what you wanted, strong and dependable, motivated to be better, no matter what life throws at me. Can you still see me, I miss you. Me and mom are still here and so is your daughter, she still misses you after all these years, I can see it in her eyes. There is so much confusion left here for me after you decided to leave this world and I cannot continue to live this way.

"Realization"

Denial has always been so forgiving when the mind begins to drift and forget the emotions which create the consequences . I began to fear your feelings as my hate engulfs you as a primary focus inadvertently leading me to this denial I have lived in for so long, a certain reality is freed from my own thoughts. I still could not fathom the change in your life, the change that did not include me. A precious love was felt within every day and every thought shared between us but so easily thrown away that love became as we drown into other realities. Tainted by life and hasty through confusion, we quickly lost that feeling that first brought us into each others arms. Your heart was a place I never wanted to leave, so warm and comforting, I slowly fell away from my own reality and began to live In yours. I was so blinded by love I thought that your reality would suffice in my life but I quickly realized the immense complications brought upon your reality. This difference between our mind states led to the end I never expected would happen as a selfish hate for you began to burn through the reality I had forgotten, my reality. Several thoughts began to race through my head as my confusion was released into your mind with desperate words of forgiveness as I felt our failure was created from my ignorance to you. I waited for understanding from your warm voice but soon realized your ignorance and discomfort was as devastating as my own. The hate began to build as the walls in our minds were replaced with a certain pain only given by one another. That perfect balance we possessed between love and hate lost all boundaries as we lost focus on the life we were trying to reach together. I tried so hard to live within your life but I lost what truly defined me as my own person. Those dreams we shared together with such a love that I thought would last forever became lost in reality and amounted to only lies from you in my mind. So my hate can only be a selfish one, twisting all of the sanity in my life creating dreams of you every night upon my restless mind leaving only an empty place in my life that will always have visions of what you once were to me and only me.

"Somewhere else"

My mind drifts into only a single thought as it always does, a single thought of only you, always you. These complications soon find reality when I begin to think about what could be, and what will be when I find the courage to make this decision I long to see an outcome from. As I dream of you every night, this feeling brings me even closer to your heart, a heart that I have to find again, a happiness only you can give me. I felt that my search was over when you fell into my life, my mind, but you had to leave, and these feelings only became stronger with time, with every thought of you gracing this troubled mind. I am so lost without you, without your voice nurturing my soul, giving me a hope that I never believed in until I met you. A question plaguing my mind every day, always new but always the same, are we meant for each other? My heart tells me that you are for me and only me but my mind always becomes blurry and distraught when I wake up to reality, a reality that I do not want to live in anymore if it does not have you, if I don't have you. Even though you are so far away, living another life, I still feel you in this one, this life I call my own. My fears overwhelms me as I know this happiness I once lived will only be a reality when I have you in my arms once again. I fear the decision that I make will not bring you back to me and I will have lost you forever leaving a bitter life that only I can live. The test of time is the only test that matters and I can only wait for you and myself to make that decision that I know will be the happiness we both long for.

"Dying with your heart"

Lying here, sleepless among the angels as I drag myself through my own mind, my own thoughts of a conclusion leading to a resolution, leading to you. Soon the dreams begin to take over reality, as every moment without you burns a scar into this lonely heart, while my life seems to drift to a place that I cannot exist in without you. It hurts so much to dream about you and to love you now that you are not here in my reality but the pain is so much easier to absorb than the thought of letting you go and ignoring the only feelings that push me through everyday. My own thoughts will soon begin to ignore me as all that will be left of me is you. Those thoughts are twisting into a state of memories, but I cannot let go despite the pain and destruction your love brings to my life. These thoughts of you are killing me over and over again as my heart lye cold in your hands. I die a little each day waiting for that certain day you will come back and upon your lips the words I long to hear, I love you. These dry tears become perfect to the touch as I run away from the reality that I must live everyday without you.

"Ungrateful"

It is so gratifying to help another, and to always seem to be there when needed, but your helpfulness always seems to go unnoticed. Just when things seem to be going the right direction, those people you always helped begin to forget all to quickly how much you have sacrificed in the past for them. Those same people forget how you pulled them out of the misery that was lived before you came about and you are left unneeded and unwanted. You wonder where they would be without you but everything must happen for a reason, or maybe you were just a sucker to be used up and forgotten. As usual, that all to familiar hate and disgust floods your veins convincing you of how much you hated those people at the beginning. So naive at the beginning, you thought that your good spirit would make things better for all that were around you but you became a pawn, used beyond your original intentions. Those ungrateful motherfuckers burn you up in the end, wasting more of a life that you could not live to begin with. You think if you help those selfish people around you that maybe a good reason for your life may show its doubtful face, but you are left used and confused. That comfortable rage soothes your mind once you realize you're tired less efforts were just a stepping stone for another ungrateful bitch. Where do you go from here, the end stays so near, but have you done what you were meant to do, or do you have to keep dragging this life behind you? Maybe you are really running from a life waiting for you to turn around and face it. You become sickened with those people's greed, you soon realize how you should not have been so blind to help them in the beginning. But where was the beginning, where do you start again? How can you start again? Silence those screams within your mind and maybe you will hear those thoughts that will bring your mind where you want it to be.

"Unfeeling"

Lifeless among these ignorant faces, I search for a reason to justify these feelings I cannot let go of. Maybe I am wrong to feel these emotion driven thoughts that lead me to one wrong decision after another. It is to late to understand these decisions after I have blindly let these emotions control my actions creating the very place that we stand in all to often which I take full responsibility for because it was I who brought us here because of these unthought out feelings. Those very feelings have left me lonely, with only those decisions I should have never made. I can only escape from reality through a love for someone that I cannot have and chemicals that are not so forgiving. This future remains clouded as I search for a resolution that may not exist in this reality. These chemicals bleed only the truth from this blackened mind but charge the price of a certain ignorance tainting the truth. I become misunderstood by those I try so hard to please, sometimes only a simple smile or response makes that decision worth feeling. Every feeling seems to have a price that I cannot pay to long after that decision is already made. I find myself pushing away those I need to be close to leaving me with only my distraught feelings of what should be or maybe only what I want to be. If I keep fighting for what I cannot have then what purpose will this life have served?

"Escape"

Let it all go, that's what you really want. Forget about all that was worked for, forget about the life that has failed you. Maybe now is the time to take that sudden change waiting for a decision only you can make, only I can make. What will become of me when all reasons for now lead to nothing, when all of the time lived for an unknown reason become wasted and forgotten? Where will I wake up tomorrow , who will I open these troubled eyes to, who will understand this complication, this misplacement of thoughts? Where will this life that I refuse to accept lead me now? So easy it would be to just leave and start over, but who remembers such a beginning? Maybe only running from my problems will create more problems leaving me with only the same reasons and decisions that have lead me here, somewhere I do not wish to be. Only a decision will lead me to where I need to be but where should I be?

"Creativity Limited"

A burning light imprints the mind with visions of ideas waiting to be thought up. Aside the urge, the ideas cant seem to form a face fast enough to feed the hunger. The paint begins to bleed through the original thought, the original canvas. Fear can be a consuming emotion when the thought of presenting your mind in a simple format defines the person living under your skin. Still you try to create that first thought on paper, on canvas. There goes that brick wall again in your mind choking your thoughts, discouraging your creativity out of fear. Why wont the thoughts just flow through your hand onto that blank piece of paper you have been lost in all night. The pen continues to be full of ink waiting to fulfill its purpose of existence much like you sit in front of this blank piece of paper waiting when you should be creating. That same paper that mocks you every night still seems to possess some kind of comfort and thought provoking power over you bringing the same situation upon each restless night. Will your thoughts ever produce an image that truly defines that complicated chain of events running through your mind? Maybe the strange comfort of sitting in front of a blank piece of paper evoking the thoughts you seem to always run from will be enough to understand what your purpose really is.

"Wearing at the threads"

Tearing at the threads, my skin seems to separate as my mind captures the thoughts of a past to far away to grasp. Finally seeing what your eldest family members have to offer, you shun your own thoughts knowing that there was a place for you in the whole ordeal. You may have lost those people in your life before, but now you realize how important playing a role in the given situation could have been. What you could have learned from the blood line that formed the very heart beating within your chest sometimes only grasping the obvious pain. That same heart beats with every breath that was taken before you. Don't forget where you come from, those same thoughts invigorate you everyday, those same people have a role in where you stand today. You had to be brought up from somewhere, your first thoughts had to have a reason, a place to start. Maybe those very thoughts supplemented a base for the structure that seems to be crumbling down now. It becomes your choice to drag an unknown bloodline through the thoughts of such a tainted soul. The thoughts, the eyes, the talent, it had to start somewhere, right? Maybe it comes out in a structure of color so close in describing the mood past down to you and only you. The obsession becomes reality when you finally come close to that idea you have been looking for, that color best surrounding a reality that you have always known. Through the lyrics of a favorite song you realize thats not right, have to try again. As the newest thoughts formulate, life rides past you again, what color will you choose now? Life doesn't wait for a single decision from you or anyone. That structure created from the very blood consuming your movement, infecting your thoughts, it waits to be destroyed and recreated. New meaning awaits as your thoughts grasp a new sense of life. Happiness fills the ancestral soul looking down upon your creative color placed within a palette outlining only what you have yet to understand.

James M Snipes

"Broken door beneath these feet"

The rain drenched windy night finds a place among this irritable day. A glimpse quickly becoming a stare as all focus becomes lost within the cracks and cringes of a simple door hinge. Its that time again, lite a cigarette, watch another lonely night drift into a made up retribution. Funny how every night seems to be a means to an end. The same emotions forbidden by society race through your mind, questioning your sanity, thought by thought. This is where the rage takes over as you begin to kick the tainted hinge, watching the door come crumbling down along with the thought of loving another. Falling to the door I see my whole existence crumbling before me. Attrition stealing your heart once again as you let the sun rise wake you into the same day that becomes lost within the same thought that lead you here to begin with.

"Ignore"

Talking to the brick wall again, expecting a response and getting the same blank stare that you have learned to accept for what it is and what it will never be. Once in love and now in denial of what you were ready to die for in the first place, what was once more than a blank face, more than the brick wall. Hope is for the blind, right? Maybe you should give it another chance or maybe you should stop talking within a moment that was already taken. A moment where I was speaking to your face and not to that gleaming face focusing on the television screen. Things are'nt always what they seem in the hands of a confused man, or woman. Asking for one thing and looking for another, how do you answer such a thing? You know the question, but the reason remains hidden within those empty statements and blank faces. Desperate for a balanced anger, a true sadness, you start to dig deep within yourself again, maybe the answer you seek is there. Or maybe the moment is long taken and the brick wall is all you will ever see in her, it is all she will ever be to you. Missing something inside still and she is gone, like the rest.

"Needing"

Its when you stop searching, an answer to the struggle of life seems to be placed right in front of you. When you finely give up on finding the face without a name, there she is, beautiful eyes, perfect smile, the angel that guided you to the point of insanity and so gracefully brings you back to the search that found you. Confusion engulfs your mind wondering if this is just another cruel joke to make you feel so weak and vulnerable. You keep your guard up just in case history decides to repeat itself once again. But, for the first time a feeling of needing is felt within your heart, not your mind. You cant live without her presence, simple thoughts are not enough, you have to be close to her no matter what you have to do to get there. You cant resist her words, her thoughts and feelings haunt you until the next time her hands rest between your own. You cant stop, the feelings within your heart control the thoughts of reality that you have become too used to. Is she real, can you really know so soon? You don't know anything about her, only a feeling that could never be replaced. You cant forget that face and you know you truly, deeply need to see her.

So, reality comes back, what do you do now? For once in your life, the heart decides over the mind. You decide to follow her to the end of the world no matter what. You realize this feeling embedded in your heart could never exist without her eyes to guide you. Fate doesn't always come at the right time but when it does, you know and feel like you cant let go and never will. To truly feel the need to be with someone does not come everyday, so when fate finds you, make sure you know what your heart is telling you and not your mind. When those eyes tell a story without a single word, you are truly looking into her soul and you will know she can be the only person to ever make you feel this way, so don't let go.

"I promise and still waiting"

I promise to always be here for you as long as you let me. I promise to be yours as long as you need me. I promise to put up with your bullshit as long as your still in my arms at the end of the night. I promise to love you when you are unsure of your own love. I promise to need you even when you don't need me. I promise to be everything you have ever dreamed of. But, I am still waiting for you to accept me, the person waiting to make your dreams come true. I am still waiting for you to face the fear that is blinding you of what is right in front of you. I am still waiting for you to realize that maybe your search for something better could end with me. Im sorry that I cant pretend this feeling deep in my heart is not real. Im sorry my feelings might be stronger than yours and it scares you. I was afraid to accept these thoughts of you taking over my mind everyday, but now that I understand this feeling I cant imagine finding it in anyone else. I have never been in this situation too, but I know I can wait for you because I feel like I have been waiting for you my whole life. I guess what Im trying to say baby is give me a chance to be the one who ends your search for something better. I know that we don't know what will happen in the future but I cant imagine having a better one without you in my life.

"Thank you"

I feel that I have to thank you because I Do not think you realize what you have done for me. You have found a person within me that I never knew was there. A person that can feel such a beautiful feeling was never the person I thought was living within me. Things seem to be moving fast between us but it just feels right, it feels good, it almost feels like fate. I have never really believed in fate but I always knew things happen for a reason. I truly look at you as an angel that stumbled into my life becoming the thing I almost gave up on finding. For once in my life, I do not feel lost, I feel complete, I feel like I would follow you anywhere just to be by your side, I feel that my fate rest in your hands, your heart. I do not mean to scare you with these feelings but I have to be true to myself and to you. I know it is happening so fast but fate never chooses a perfect time and it never waits for us to grasp the happiness placed in front of us. I know the situation can become complicated and I am willing to see where our hearts will lead us with a certain fear that I may loose you. I cant imagine even after a short time together how I could live my life without seeing your beautiful face everyday of my life. We have both been in love with others in life and have learned from those mistakes and enjoyed those moments that make life worth living. It is so hard for me to explain in words how I feel about you because I have never felt so intoxicated while in the presence of a single person. I have never felt a single breath within a crowded room like I feel yours. I have always been very aware of what and who is around me but when I am close to you and looking into your eyes I feel nothing but you flowing through my mind and body bringing me a peace that I never thought I would feel. Your words soothe my tensions in life and your touch soothes my ever busy mind, you bring a peace to me that I dont think I could ever find in anyone else. When I am with you I forget about all of the negative things that have always consumed my life, the things that have controlled my thoughts for so long. You bring me a certain sense of hope, a feeling that never could be replaced and never be let go of.

"Sorrow for eyes of the hopeful"

Have you ever been so lost within yourself, running away is not an option? To fall into the comfort of sleep only brings the same dream of the same face haunting you? A confusion so real created through a love between two people, and it only brings an end you were so sure would never happen. You finely let your guard down and place every hope into a single soul, just to be pushed away once again. Tragedy surrounds your life from every place close to you and the closest thing just lets go despite a beautiful love shared between the both of you. Hurt is a normal cycle in your life but this pain is one without a solution, one without a reason to feel. You finally let go of that fear always holding you back because deep within you is a new trust, something you are so sure about. And when you find the fought within these feelings among the other tragedies filling your mind, nothing except death wants to show its comfort and simplicity. Time loses every meaning of human design when your life only sees a thought, a vision, time loses all of the value and purpose it has ever served. Time is not healing the pain the way it always has, you have lost any concept of hope or need. You cant see time and you cant see reality, only a face buried so deep within you, what else would be worth seeing, just her face. What else would be worth giving every part of you except for that beautiful face haunting you every moment of every breath you become more thankful to breath. You found her after giving up on looking and though the time is wrong, time just lost every virtue it ever had. The pain is waiting for time to heal it but for the first time this hurt is buried so deep, a reason can not be found. I miss her body next to mine, I miss every moment I smiled just from a simple gesture. There is nothing better than the feeling of a love you felt so sure of coming from another heart. I cant let go of something I put my soul into because she still has every part of me in her hands and that is a trust never to be given to another. Just want to hold her face and keep her heart near. I just need her near, every part of her. Cant live without her, cant live in this pain. So what options have you, live or die? Though you feel completely dead inside now, physical life must come back. Now is the time when all of that hurt in your life finally has a purpose, a reason. She brought you to the deepest part of your soul and made you realize the strength that has always been there, buried waiting to be needed. For this you must love her the only way you can for the moment and hope those deep seeded feelings will be the reality you are still longing for.

"At the bottom of sadness"

Falling in love with a dream as always. Searching for that last face you held before having to wake up to reality once again. Living through pain after pain, finally you have fallen to the bottom of your soul. And what do you find, only a sadness so naturally brought from the pain that has always placed every step you have made. The deepest trust was given from the deepest part of you and irony takes meaning when you realize she was the one to show you that part of you that was never given the chance to be let out. Guilt has no place in life when we all make such mistakes but we all seem to take blame for others actions in our lives. Two people feel so much hurt for hurting each other which could only lead to a love that will always be. So much worry left between you both. Still needing someone you know you will always be waiting for. How can you pick yourself up from the bottom you were happy to finally find? Cant forget the person that helped you find that part of you. In your heart holds a trust that knows your roads will cross again, but when? What can you do while waiting, should you still be waiting? Maybe you should move on, but how to move on when you are so sure of what and who you are waiting for? Such a confusion yields to no single answer, no single reason. The whole point will be missed if only one simple truth stands out in your mind. You are standing too deep within yourself now to still be searching for an easy way out of these newly found feelings. You cant escape yourself once you finally learn who has been hiding under the skin for all of these years. Truly a wonderful feeling it is to love someone from the bottom of your very soul. Don't forget that the one you love was the only one to let you feel who and what you really are inside. So here comes that dreaded reality again waking up every sense in your mind, even the ones you thought died long ago. The pain your life has always been defined by begins to flood through every part of you, haunting you, twisting you to a point where you must purge and release all of this energy building inside. You always knew that loneliness would be at the end of this struggle, you always knew that she would not remain in your arms no matter how much you love her. You always knew the next chapter in your life would be starting from now. Yet a spirit seems to flow through you when walking through familiar places. Something seems to still grasp your heart reminding you of a love you cannot pretend to forget. Some things will always remain buried within the heart and they may never be true again but within those moments of trust and love, a certain feeling of yourself was discovered and will never be forgotten. Pain will follow you through every door you ever decide to open but to feel such a love and such an understanding of yourself is the only happiness you will ever find with the worth of what life should feel like.

"Empty ring finger"

Empty heart worn through a symbol of a life once lived upon that sacred finger, the sweetest truth ever changing without reason. In search again, a beautiful face, a new smile, there she is again taking your every breath, taking over your thoughts. One word changing the perspective you learned to accept around you. One action from your steps through a fragile reality show a promise for the reality that was looking for us both all along. Truth and honesty, two impossible things to find in a person these days but we both are searching for the same. Hidden smile upon your busy eyes walking through a place you have grown to hate. Drowning myself in chemicals I find a certain motivation in myself to find that drive, that burning emotion that I strive for. Something in you finding a place in myself, something I cant deny.

"Fucking ridiculous"

Man preying on man, religion defining a reason to kill another man out of an ignorant single belief of one righteous being. Political figures gaining power as we lay powerless against a power we all created to feel safe. The fault of human nature is to destroy what we have created in turn gaining a belief that we all remain safe within a single thought of a single being. Humans love the excuse of other humans as to why we are what we are from single views of situations we all pretend to understand. This is the part I blame an ex love for my fuck ups but I cannot possibly hold her responsible when every decision I made was out of my own creations and destructions of my own being. The world crumbles these days at the first site of money lost, currency created in fear years ago. People empowering unjust causes against other people to satisfy a meaningless venture...for what, what fucking reason could another human possibly have to imprison another person within a system that didn't work from the start? Anyone ever think that our time is running thin, maybe we are not almighty as we would portray ourselves to be. There is much more out there than the simple narrow viewed life we all call our own. Humans long to control other humans, nature, politics, thoughts, lives, systems built through fear to gain the highest currency to pay for what? Money will always create a false sense of control over the people just like you and me.

"Just a smile"

Such a fool I could be to chase such a beautiful smile, a fictional face on a bright screen begging my attention. Such a fool I am to dream of that smile, that beautiful energy found in the simplest yet sweetest of words. What to understand among my thoughts of a beautiful soul I have yet to meet, could she be what I search for? Every thought finds a question, a long for reason to put the puzzle back to what I want it to be. Could my search end in a smile or maybe it will begin with your smile, question is why do my thoughts continue to follow the smile of a beautiful stranger?

"Still Reaching"

Grabbing that which never found a reality within any heart. Making true that which we all knew was a lie from the start. Such a fool to reach for an empty reality, a truth never to find its own path. Yet I still reach for a dream only brought on through chemicals and a desperate loneliness instead of the dream that has been true to me all along. It seems just human nature to long for what cannot and will never be instead of the final happiness staring us through every site we think may be a new truth. Denial, the sweetest excuse to just let go of the very thing we needed all along in exchange for a cheap thrill to satisfy a craving that will only expire at the end of the night.

"Strength is your weakness"

Physical energy burning through every wall you face with a price you refuse to pay as your strength will guide you past the reason you need to see. Force it through, destroy all that stands in front of your perceived you...another reason to miss the point of your very existence. Cannot reason with passion, you may think your wrong but feel right and will use brute strength to prove that point if even its just for yourself. Such a selfish nature any strength can have and be. Such rage within confusion always finding the same conclusion, a feeling of weakness for not controlling a temper you have lived with for so long. Still brute anger brings the ultimate conclusion despite your destruction along the way. Again your lack of patience proves your mental view of any situation proving to only you that waiting is only a waist of time. Question is what did you miss upon your path of rage?

"To die is to think"

A day within a week I find a time to die inside through chemicals. In that day I find peace, frustration, need and a certain want to be with you in my last breaths hoping you will bring me back yet I have yet to learn your name. I guess the chemicals play their part as you do in this mental parody I call my life. First moments thought out to a certain end within the very moment my eyes meet yours. Thoughts become a curse when my own prevent those little things that mean the most in life. So I die a bit each week to find a new start, a new reason to think or simply a new person to be. I see now there is never a new person behind the over thought out judgments I have made in my life. The thoughts are me and the judgments are the person I never wanted to be. We all try to change what is when we should be understanding why we are standing where we don't want to be.

Outside of thought

How ideal things should be outside of my own thoughts. Perfect smiles, blind happiness, should I buy into the deception? Maybe just rebellious thoughts I feel now, maybe a simple kind heart as your own would keep me on the path I have always longed to follow. Problem is my thoughts as long as I allow them to be will never let me follow such a path...any path. Every thought pattern has a conclusion,one I cannot find, not on my own. Should I sacrifice my thoughts for the conclusion you could find in me? Should I allow you to renew my purpose in the absence of thought? Will I follow this dream once again, same dream, different face, different story, different beauty.

"Letting go"

Loving you, missing you, but your not there anymore. Living a dream, grasping a heart that is only real in this mind. Making every step but still landing in those imaginary arms once again. Thoughts become drowned in tears with only your hand to cling to but your not here anymore. Loving you for reasons still unseen to these eyes. Knowing you have left me, I cant leave you, I cant leave the thoughts of you filling my days and tormenting my nights. Lying in this bed, feeling you though your body is not next to mine, feeling something that may never be again. You have moved on and so have I but these thoughts buried so deep seem to embrace this mind no matter what step I take away from you. The further I walk away from you, the closer I find myself close to those simple thoughts of you, that smile, that expression on your face every time I spoke. I remember our last kiss, that feeling of letting go, it was the hardest thing that I ever had to do. And when you told me goodbye, every breath within this tainted body stopped and I really don't think I remember how to breath. My life found meaning in you and now my life seems to find an end in you. Im trying to start from that but your face always seems to be at the end. The same memories race through my mind everyday, the same thoughts, nothing has changed inside. I thought that time always heals the broken heart, I thought not seeing your beautiful face everyday would let me forget but I was wrong once again.

"After more in nothing"

Falling through a time without a reason to exist, touch becoming as simple as a dream yet lived nor felt. Needing what has already been and will only be for the reason you still struggle to understand. Purpose still losing reason within the very reality chosen before choice was an option. Always the eyes, so many beautiful eyes, so many beautiful women, all with a purpose without a beginning nor an end. Without focus, without you, without her, cannot see, cannot feel, another faceless reason, another empty purpose. To understand is to know, to know is to feel, to feel is to find a real purpose, a true reason to create the very actions you live throughout others in hopes of making a difference within another life but hope will only slow you down. We all want more than we have blinding us to the beauty of what is, what is in front of us and what we are and will only be.

"All we will ever have"

Our past loves, ourselves, the closest and the furthest. The living, the dead, both exist in some memory, some love, some life. Looking for her, for him, they were always there. Emotion, lust, love, all found within the same being. Once found, your end found a cure for the sadness, it was always you. Loving, missing, the answer is always within. You only miss what you cant have, you only love what you miss. Our search always ends in ourselves, where it all began. What reason do we stand in such a place we know will only fade, why do we pick a path we know will end in ourselves? Maybe life is only a search within ourselves serving a purpose for every heart we touch along the way. Love, a chemical imbalance in the mind, hate, an ignorant view of what we have yet to understand. The furthest emotions will always find a home within those uncertain thoughts of what we all think life should be. Were only missing the people we missed the chance to have. Don't miss the people that will always find a memory of what you could only find in the end of yourself.

"Almost"

So close, I was right there and you were one more touch away from dragging me down that endless road of chemical driven feelings that are so conveniently called love. Was it just another fake smile or maybe a time not ready to be lived? Such a thought wondered is the one I almost always have in my grasp. Just another page in my book, just another planned moment I thought would develop into a new reality. A blank perception once again has blinded me to the lingering existence of my loneliness. Wishful thinking it is so simply called to thrive for the one thing you will never have though its very essence insures a breath from your wasted body every morning you wake to live yet another day with the same ending you dread living. Alone again in this bed, this pattern of thought bringing me to this place, the same conclusion to every game I would rather not play. What purpose could there be in this illusion of happiness when my dreams find the reality I long for? Will these words ever stumble upon the path that will make this life the one I should be living.

"Beautiful mess"

Walking upon a simple gesture of what we could have been, what I still need us to be. What reasons could possibly hold a truth so real as the very thought of you following my mind and its intentions. You decide for me before I understand the reasons for my decision already made. You fill my mind within every step and conclusion I find for every situation. What a beautiful mess we find in the very feelings drawing us back to each other when we only want everything outside of the feelings we always consider a beautiful mess. How can such a beautiful person keep stumbling upon this mess I consider a life? I found a life without you to only see your face at the end of every dream I had for this new found life. The struggle of purpose seems to lead us both within a point of sleeplessness upon the very attraction we found in us.

"Bending into place"

Crumbling grounds upon the very place we fought to stand upon. Holding those so close just to watch them fall beyond your reach. I found the point of a perfect life just to realize perfection is the same illusion we all live by within every breath we cant thank another for. I found a grasp for that perfect love just to watch her drift beyond that crumbling existence I call my life. Family, friends, that solid ground I loved so much falls from me as I see the truth, we create every step, every solid ground we choose to call home. I found her in my darkness and all along I could only find the truth about myself through the light she so gracefully gave me. Drifting angels, honest demons giving the best reasons to just give in. Temptation, realization, every reason in hand to give it all up just to release the urge we all keep buried deep inside. I tried to keep you buried deep within a place I would never visit again but you seem to find a place in my every thought and it seems I have found the true meaning of not being able to live without someone. It seems I will never truly exist the way Im meant to without you in my arms....Dreaming and wanting.

"Climbing, grasping, begging"

At the bottom of your sadness a new person seems to forget the original mind buried within. Finally reaching the deepest point just to find a replacement for who you already are. So you find yourself searching once again but her face still seems to control every step you make only leading back to her in some way. Almost leaving her in the back of your mind, that voice is heard again after all this time and everything comes back to mind like it was never absent at all. To begin again seemed so simple after just making that decision but those old feelings remain to be new ones. Time remains to be a useless attribute in this life as this love doesn't seem to fade. You are still climbing and clawing from the bottom of yourself with the thought of a new beginning. What is the first face you see once you drag yourself from that endless pit of struggle, her, the angel never leaving your mind, never leaving the grasp in your mind. Reaching the top of the new you, she still seems to be buried deep within you. But she isn't dragging you down, only remaining to be the end of your search. So, why are you still searching exactly, maybe she is searching and you are simply waiting for her to see what is right in front of those eyes. Those beautiful eyes still guide the path you seem to keep stumbling into. Life is ever changing with only one thing remaining the same, your feelings felt so deep within, those feelings only for her. You believe with every part of your soul that a love is still felt between the both of you but a certain fear seems to keep you an ocean away from those arms. What are you waiting for, go to her. There is a great happiness at stake, follow your heart, the only way she showed you to follow it. Follow her to the end of the world or yourself, fulfill that promise you made to only her. The heart in mind controls every step, every breath, every love you choose to pursue. Leave the fear for the end and follow what you feel must be done now. We control our own time, we create the very lives lived between us, happiness is but a choice away, just have to find the strength to make the most important choice of your life. That strength remains at the bottom of your sadness, waiting to be accepted.

"Empty Romance"

New face, new chance without choice. So many face's so little choice, feelings without reason, love without an end. So many choices without the chance to understand a feeling. Where will this love find an end, a heart to accept, to love the same? Destiny can only be a choice hidden in fear, a choice no one can make, fate as they call it. Choosing your destiny ends in the feelings you felt without reason so choice seems to have a limit of truth. To fall in love cant be a choice, but a reason to feel what you want so much deep inside to feel, a means to an end. Love seems to only serve as a game, a reason to think, a reason to ignore the reality around you. What purpose will you find in your reason when love will always find an end? A life without love may be a clearer one but what is a life without feeling, without happiness, without meaning. Does meaning define purpose or does reason find you through another, through another love? Will you see past reason to feel love or will you strive for an empty purpose? Only a question life seems to produce, only a simple reason to even exist but then love comes in finding another purpose in you. We all seem to exist in an empty romance through a reality forced upon our eyes, our very thoughts. What purpose will your reality find when love finds you? Will love be your reason or your purpose or maybe it will only be a chapter along your journey for a better you. Whatever the reason, your reality will always be the same.

"Every moment remembered"

As I climb these stairs every night I remember her first walking up these very stairs, I still wonder of that first impression set upon her mind. She fell right into my eyes, walking past the distractions I place in my everyday vision to forget a past that I should have learned from by now. I guess im not smart enough to stop falling in love yet as my guard fell to the ground when first feeling her hands upon my skin. Those eyes pulled me into a new world from the beginning and there was nothing I could do to change the path I became a part of. I wanted to fight this feeling away but these feelings within my heart took me over before I knew who was really standing in front of me. Once I realized the face within my grasp, this love inside found a true feeling of needing. I wasnt ready to meet her, the angel in my mind, but there she was, my whole life changed within the single moment I met her eyes with my own. I didn't want this but in time I felt that I needed it and maybe I still do. Every evil part of my very being came out to her but she seemed to love every part, good and bad. She was the first to grasp and love every part of me, how ironic she feels that her love isn't enough, it was more than I could ever dream of having, again. But it seems the moments are all I have now to hold when I beg for a peaceful rest every night alone in my bed longing for her touch. My heart denies my thoughts when I choose to stop believing in love, I cant escape what pushes me through everyday of this confused life. I don't want to love, I don't want to feel this warm killing pain within but the moments of past always remind me of the love I must still be feeling to be drowning in the same thoughts I knew before I knew her. I remember our last moments, when she walked to the plane, I could feel her taking my heart with every step she made away from me, further she drifts, but closer I feel her. Moments go by, days go by, I can only feel her still, I can only live the moments with her that defined my life into what it has become. I found the life long dream in her, happiness. What can I do once my search found an end? My life was a search for myself, for her, I found both in a moment. Maybe I didn't say enough, maybe I said too much, its too late now. Maybe the time is wrong, but none of us ever pick the right time to feel. I wish I could walk across this ocean to feel your lips again, just one more time, just to know these feelings inside are real. I wish I could be standing in front of your door right now just to see the smile on your face, the smile I miss creating. To hold your body against mine would remind me that Im still breathing, it would remind me of the reasons I still seem to be in love with you. You will never get away from my love as I will never get away from myself. I want to move on with my life, but you are all that will ever complete this life. So, now I stand here within a dream of change but my dream was found in you.

"Every Thought"

Always leading to the same sadness this life will always live. She cannot be the only reason your tears are becoming the only comfort within your longing sleep. It was your heart that was given, it was your choice. Cant blame another for choices made through feeling. Hope will always find its end within a reality of truth. To hope only brings a weakness, you cant hope for what you truly desire in this life. We must step over hope to grasp the person standing within, it was always there, waiting. Sadness always wrapping a certain comfort around me but I always find myself trying to break through the ease of comfort. Im always trying to find a way out of the very place I stand now, never seems to be enough. Always searching, always hoping, then you realize once again that hope will only bring hurt. Don't hope, grasp the truth that decides to show its face and hold the truth that seems to always be buried within your very soul. No one will ever tell you what is truly within, you have to feel it to know that it may be real and you have to feel another to know that it is truly real within every thought you have known and will ever think. I guess that I will never find another to take your place but I realize that place in my heart could only hold your heart. Maybe it will never change, no reason to forget a love that only you will bring from me. If it was only for once, I know it was at least possible from this bleeding mind. I see now that love holds many meanings. I hold much love and much hate, it seems to be your face that makes all confusion disappear, all questions answered in a single breath. I will never forget your eyes bringing me the peace that I was dying for everyday. I finally found my angels name in you and your confusion brought my own to an end. I hope it will find your resolution, I hope my ending will find your beginning. I guess hope is useless when a strong mind can find a reason for a decision already made.

"Faceless smiles"

Unanswered promises, looking for her in yet another smile, another promise of a happy ending. Those lips, that smile, ignore the face and maybe you can pretend its her even if its just for a moment before reality passes. Those sweet lips are so inviting but the eyes don't tell the story you hoped would end in that smile. New face, new life, same feelings of something waiting to fade. You found a bigger smile, one that makes all in her presence smile without reason but she only opened your reality to see in your own eyes, your own story. The same feelings remain with a new smile to guide you into your new reality. Falling back in love with an old face, an old story. Falling out of love again, she moved on through you, without you. Your own eyes forget the story, the reason, forgot how to see the reality you let surround your every thought of what happiness should be. Losing a place to stand, losing a happiness to grip, to believe in, to cherish for what it is and could be, the very ground you stand upon loses merit when trust becomes a game. Selfish words, thoughtless actions, old promises fade through out a whispering wind, old words, new feelings. Everything begins to twist again through out your words but who are you to me, who am I to you? Lost we may be but what brings us to the same point every time? A love, a lust, something means something in this place, we seem to keep finding each other in the same place. What will we mean to each other in this place? Who will we be at the end of this story? What purpose does love serve when time will always steal anything that was ever worth feeling or being or having? It cant be better to love and loose when love will always end without meaning, without the purpose of a beginning.

"Following Hearts"

Finding a life in you and living one without you. New interest, new smiles, always leading to the same lonely night I have learned to love too well. Complications in her smile, standing in another place, finding another place within the same smile of a beautiful face only leading to the same point of regret. Losing a place to stand within the moments I decided to follow my own heart. So left without an obvious choice, I followed you to another end I thought would be our new beginning. Maybe I was wrong to drive you to this point but you were wrong to leave me like this. I thought our love found its purpose but I guess we still follow the path disguised as a search. A moment ended in us, was it really the end of our search within each other? This cant be the end between us, I love you too much to say goodbye so soon, our purpose is still waiting for us. This part of me needs you so much but maybe it isn't right or maybe it is, all I know is you have remained within my heart from the start so I will follow you and us until our road ends where it should.

"Hidden faces"

Your so loving in my dreams but so distant in your reality. So close in a moment but so far away within this lifetime. I always knew our roads would cross again but it seems so much has changed in our lives since that first feeling was felt between us. You remain untouchable within the moments I need your touch the most, your words bringing me so close just to push me away when our skin can finally find the path to one another. I cant see past the deep suggestions from your heart, do you really want me or is this confusion something we still share after all this time? Your heart remains within mine after these years of trial and hardship, who has been the most tainted at this point? A story to tell, a life to live, the path will always pick us before we could possibly choose a way to walk the path, at this point...creating a path of this life could be the only option. Such love will always reach an end, the bottom before it will reach the point which always seems to be the end, it seems an ending always starts the beginning you only wanted an ending for from the start. Sublime in the fact of glory but did I really win anything?

"It has to end now"

Through a simple gesture I blindly gave you my heart again with thoughts of us being together the way we should be, again I was wrong about you. The lies soon followed your empty promises of a future I always thought we would end in. I was blind again to trust your true intentions. I was lying to myself with thoughts of your true ambition and dedication to what we could be together. You became a game that I can no longer play, a precious memory I guess I will have to leave in the past. Why would you open my heart to you again when you never meant to be with me from the start?

"Just to be forgotten"

Another relationship, another smile, with what purpose... with what reason have you found your own smiles in my chaos? Physical purity enjoyed within every breath until expired through memories too soon to be forgotten. I became your answer within a moment just to be forgotten within a second when you realized my direction would only find truth in you. The memory factory hard at work bringing smiles of a perfect time and perfect smiles induced through chemicals leaving a trail of memories soon to be forgotten. A simple kiss, a simple love affair, none worth a simple memory. A journey within new found friends can take us to the highest point until reality sets in sending us spiraling down to the reality just waiting to expose who we really are behind the chemicals.

"New memories and old feelings"

In front of you once again, the same chaos as before, moments you thought would never occur again. Pointless words screaming through my mind again from your silent whispers. Your words cutting through my every thought, no logic, no reason to remain in this state of denial. The same questions about you will never find an answer at this point. You will never see the reality before this point.

"Really"

Wasted time, beautiful schemes to end a night and begin a search of that media driven reality we all crave from time to time. What the fuck were you thinking, a phone call, a single flirt could bring you the pointless sex we all need leaving that empty promise at the end of the bed? Longing for that which comes natural but finding nothing once we find ourselves in the arms of a stranger clinging to the same illusion of an instant happiness. The same word leads your thoughts, really, did I just fall for her within a drunken smile, an influenced circumstance? Restart, another night, another thought pattern, another drunken smile leading you to the same empty choices you decide not to make this time around but make up for it with the delusion that this one might be real. Really, did you learn the first ten fucking times? A women with one thing you loved dearly came around and put you in the same place you are now dreaming of a way out. Or maybe it's the way in which you want bad so much to denie who you really are at the end of the day.

"Ruins"

Among the desolate mind new thoughts emerge to create a new way of thought, another system of denial for the one heart you wish to consume. Single thoughts and short messages within breaths of wanting create a love so true and so real..let me love you my dear, I cannot let you down. Meaning without words and words without reason but still screaming a truth of what we should be. Where do I place you in my heart, where will you rest among these thoughts of honesty and comfort ? How long will I wait to run my fingers through your hair, down your face...feel those lips upon my own? How much should I love you before the chance is given to hold you close to a heart full of wanting and frustration? When will my love for you find truth in your untrusting ways and denial of what should be? Loving a ghost while In search of a free spirit locking every door I step in front of in hopes of my angel standing right there with open arms. So close within your breath upon my face, sad tears from your warm skin complimenting the warm smile I long to create everyday of the beautiful life I feel Im meant to bring you.

"Screaming Silence"

Falling out of love into another time of silence. Losing her while trying to find another. A decision to grasp her pain upon your own only brings anger and regret. It seems you were strong enough to take away any regret she had in breaking your heart but your own pain shadows any reason she could of had to let go of the one person waiting a lifetime to meet her. Time bleeds into reality as it should but thoughts and feelings of her stay deep without reason. In search of comfort and forgetfulness, her face seems to keep emerging into every silence. Grasping the empty blackness, her skin finds its way within your hands once again. A time without words, such a long time to not hear that precious voice but those last words scream through every word that you manage to speak. Old memories and empty walls surround you while walking through a familiar place. Feeling her as a ghost when only standing next to the place you held her, the place you kissed her and loved her. An ocean away still but you can almost feel her next to you through a screaming silence within an empty room filled with only memories. It seems these words to you have always been from me, for me, to me but always for those with a broken heart. The point of my words has no ending, only a love that will always find itself within her heart. This silent mind screams for her but when the screams will not return an answer, it is time to move on, everything has an end in some way, just not always the ending we were looking for. Look, love and live, its all we will ever have.

"Simple attachments"

Drawn to you for reasons I will never understand. Your sheer beauty attracts my physical eye but your energy grabs my heart within every glance your eyes fall upon my own. Trying to find you within a moment but losing you within a heartbeat. I try to forget you through time but something in your words, in that smile always brings me back to these thoughts of you, of what we may be. Between the mirror my eyes only seem to find you with an even lapse in time between feeling your heart and losing your attention in the same grasp. I thought I would have let go of you a long time ago but a simple attachment brings the idea of you back to this lonely heart holding a place for the ghost that is you.

"Symbol of Power"

Once man reaches the top of the mountain he will climb yet another to fulfill that inherited human trait of control and power. Once that man runs out of mountains to conquer he reverts back to his very nature and destroys those very accomplishments in order to gain more currency, more power, just to feed the urge. People, humans would rather stick their heads in the sand and pretend to live a perfectly normal life instead of accepting the very human traits that others use to control us through the fear of truth. It seems a systematic control was born many years ago in order to keep us all at bay, keep us without informed opinions. So easy to point the finger at the governments but the truth is men of wealth become men of power whether they want it or not. Sure government manipulates the system to control simple people but the men of power buy the government to serve a single agenda. A single agenda spawns many to the cause of control as long as the pay off fits the idea.

"The love that never was"

Around your thoughts my mind twist among boundaries put up out of the common fear of a real happiness. I begin to question my illusion of you, am I dreaming, are you just a soul produced through my constant wishful thinking? Did I find you in a dream and just go with it..convinced myself what we had was truly real and able to grow into something worth having? Am the fool here to believe in a thought, a simple voice, an attachment through technology? Did I fall in love with a face never held, eyes never gazed upon, a smile never kissed? Did I let my guard down after all this time just to look for a stronger point in myself? Did I find myself in the fictional perception of her, of you that I hold dear or did I simply find a reason to be stronger? Have I found what could be love once again or just a perpetual hole I continue to dig? Does my heart ache from a true pain or a desperate attempt to feel something? Will you ever awake by my side, will I ever touch your heart through your skin, will I ever know the you I feel should be or maybe Im just living from that wishful thinking I still believe to be true? Did I dream of you, did you find me, why does your ghostly face haunt me so? You let me go out of fear as I hold you out of a blind wanting. Are you afraid to be happy, are you in fear of what I might do? Is trust such a wasted dream to you that Im just a fantasy that could never be real despite the fact Im still standing here in front of you? Will I ever find you in my arms or have I gone to far past that point you were looking to fulfill? You say I am so much to you but you cant even make the time to see me...you live on impulse when Im right here waiting to be next to you. Your fears have no place in this heart baby, if you want me Im waiting, if not I can only hope you found peace in my words....I may not be much but Im all yours if thats what you really want.

"Your mystery"

Clever thoughts portray your eyes within every conversation we begin to have. Something in you captured me but only a small part of you I can even begin to feel. Displaying such a fake character yet giving me another real piece of you every moment I can feel you in my arms. What is it you search for in me fore I cannot read you leading me to a want to know you. Much time these eyes have fallen into yours with returned smiles and conversation but I find myself ever searching for your purpose in my life as well as mine to yours. I cannot take you lightly into my heart as you have brought me many of those little moments that seem to matter most in life. I find myself longing for those simple moments we share between the bar as it's the only chance you give me to see those wondering eyes. It feels as if I have known you for a lifetime yet never have I met you face to face away from distraction. I await a point and a reason as to why I feel the need to see you and why I look forward to a simple hug, a simple touch from you when I am always wanting more.

"Throw this life away"

Submerged in a time less lived through alcohol and lost loves. Surrounding yourself in those close enough to feel who you really are but in between those wonderful times, your drinking again just to find sleep. It seems peace is found before sleep and confusion holds your hand once again when your eyes finally lose focus. Energy burns through you looking for a purpose even in rest. Rage, anger, love, where to stand, what to believe? Who to stand by, who to love, why to love them? What will you stand for when a time of ignorance controls the most powerful politician which always felt a control upon you. Screaming for answers without questions, you missed the moment, you missed her. Such hands grow cold while finding the purpose to love her, the very reason to find her again. Thoughts collide within a moment, every rage, every love twisted through a single time of truth. Blood drenched sadness, hate flooding through your veins pushing for an opening. Your mind bursting through silent words never finding the surface that was always so close but your trembling hands never could grasp that one second of breath. Those seconds, so precious, so beautiful, breathing still held no option. After your faint goodbye to her, breathing started to fall into place once again for a short period before missing her. Desperately trying to look past the beginning and end of one person that will always be one within you, the words lose a place in time as time loses a place in you. Throw this life away but she is still there in your beginning and end, so where are you now, your beginning or end?

"When my darkness finds your light"

Burning souls without reason without purpose without site. Such a dream our words seem, two souls bound for truth in search of guidance from each other though guidance has never been a strong point for either of us. Dredging through that dark place in hopes of a new light but once again hope is something we will never find truth in. Blind truths and useless gestures, will we ever find a purpose, a reason to be? Will we ever find each other?

"Have we met"

Dreams and thoughts between us so twisted among your understood thoughts of uncertainty. Where would our hearts be without the words we seem to share every morning and every night...where would we be now? I find myself looking for a future without you but I cant imagine such a place now where my angel doesn't touch upon my every thought leading to my every action through out everyday of my life. Where could I be without you, how could this life breath without the purpose of meeting you face to face, my trembling hands upon your doubtful face? That smile finally mine to hold without obstacle without the wall you put up, the wall I climb everyday to reach you. How I dream of that day, you and me...hand to hand..smile to smile...your lips kissing my own as we always wanted. Where will we be after that day we both long for so dearly?

"Does the cycle ever end"

Fall in love, loose a dream, find a smile...all beginnings as well as endings. Attraction, conversation, love, dreams found and lost within the lifetime of a moment. Painful mistakes and kind resolutions never found in the same heart. Smiles and words, both the key to that life long pursuit of happiness but life works in cycles not findings. Dreams realized, houses bought and cookie cutter lives set in place, where will you turn when the eventual boredom sets in? Most just start another cycle before ending the last without a thought, reason or even a true explanation of their actions. Broken hearts never to be accounted for, paths never to find an end but sure to find a place in the new cycle of a madness that we all call life.

Live your dreams, love your findings and be thankful for every breath you are blessed to breath as you never know when your cycle will end. Nothing last forever no matter how much you believe it will, reality is as harsh as it can be helpful. Love is a blinding misconception of reality leading to lives we always thought we wanted to live until another natural attraction finds its way in your narrow line of sight. It is human nature to love as much as it is to hate that which we will never understand because we choose to be ignorant to the obvious. However choice is a misguided right we pretend to have knowing deep down we are almost programmed from birth to live and love in what can be a narrow minded view of a simple parents observation of moments past in a different time. Happiness will always find itself in the moments we are too busy to enjoy as we are always looking for a better one.